*Painting on Silk*

# Images of Africa

*Zarza*

*SEARCH PRESS*

First published in Great Britain 1992
Search Press Limited,
Wellwood, North Farm Road,
Tunbridge Wells,
Kent TN2 3DR

English translation copyright © Search Press
Limited 1992

Originally published in France
by Dessain et Tolra, Paris

Copyright © Dessain et Tolra 1991

Translated by Giles de la Bedoyère

Photographs by Thierry Fontaine

If you have any difficulty in obtaining any of the materials or equipment
mentioned in this book, then please write for further information to the
publishers: Search Press Ltd., Wellwood, North Farm Road, Tunbridge
Wells, Kent TN2 3DR

There are references to the use of solvents in this book.
These substances should be handled with care.

- All solvents should be kept in sealed containers out
  of the reach of children.

- Solvents are poisonous.
  Do not inhale vapours.

- Solvents are highly inflammable.
  Do not smoke when using them.

- Work in a well-aired room and wear plastic gloves.

ISBN 0 85532 742 1

Composition by Genesis Typesetting, Laser Quay, Rochester, Kent
Printed in Spain by Elkar S. Coop.

# Contents

# Enlarging a design

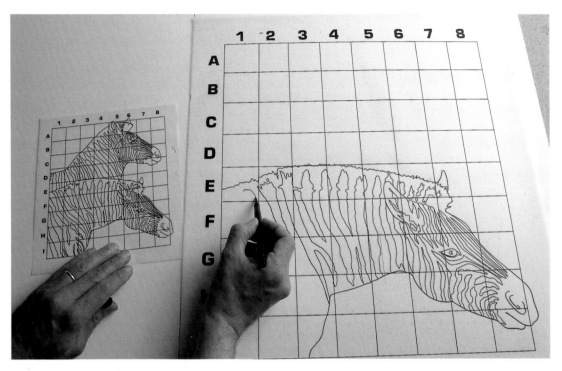

Most design ideas, including those given in this book, cannot be transferred directly on to the silk as they are too small. The simplest way of enlarging the design is to use a photocopier, but this has its limitations. The professional method illustrated here can be used to produce any size, but requires a little patience.

Divide the original motif into squares with horizontal and vertical lines to produce a grid, marking the squares with letters and numerals, as shown. Take a piece of paper to give the design size you require and divide this in the same way. Reproduce the lines of the original drawing in the same position, and to the correct proportions, in the larger squares. When all the lines have been transferred, even out any slight irregularities along the dividing lines of each square.

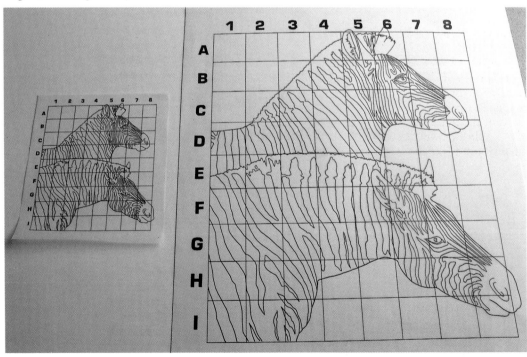

# Materials

## Applicator for gutta

A small container made of soft plastic can be obtained for applying gutta to the silk. Cut off the tip of the bottle and insert a metallic stylographic nib, as shown here. These come in different thicknesses, from the finest, No. 1 measuring about one-tenth of a millimetre, to the largest, No. 10, one millimetre. A beginner is advised to use a 0.6mm, then having mastered the application of gutta, a 0.4mm.

Fill the applicator with gutta, close the top and press the bottle to release a steady and continuous flow of gutta through the hollow pen nib, see the gutta technique explained on page 10.

*Storing the applicator*
Take an airtight jar with a secure lid and pour in a little benzine or lighter fuel, then place the applicator in the jar and close the lid firmly. The evaporation of the solvent will prevent the gutta from drying out and enable you to reuse the applicator indefinitely. The nibs will also clean themselves in the fluid.

## Brushes

Watercolour brushes are best for painting on silk as they can hold plenty of diluted paint to cover background areas, but also come to a fine point for delineating details. You will also need a very fine brush for minute details.

Brushes with sponge heads are useful for covering large areas and you can also use a ball of rolled-up cotton wool for this purpose.

# Silk fabrics

A very wide range of silk fabrics is available, some of which are easy to paint on and others which are more difficult. The following information will help you to choose the type most suitable for your purpose.

### Pongé No. 5

A light, pliable and inexpensive silk, suitable for the beginner and ideal for scarves. It adapts well to the application of gutta and shows up the design clearly.

### Pongé No. 7

A thicker fabric than No. 5, useful for cushions and lampshades but still fairly easy for a beginner to handle.

### Pongé Nos. 9 and 10

The thickest of this type of fabric, with a dense weave. Suitable for most garments, large decorative panels and cushions.

### Twill

This fabric is distinguished by lines of diagonal fluting and is a very popular choice for all garments. As it is quite thick, you must make sure that any gutta is applied on both sides.

### Honan, wild silk

This type of silk is produced by using a natural thread of irregular thickness which gives it a rustic appearance. The delineation of contour lines is much more difficult to obtain on this kind of surface. For this reason, it is advisable to limit the application of gutta and concentrate instead on colour effects and contrasts.

### Crêpe de Chine

This can be used as given for a thick pongé. Crêpe does, however, absorb a greater quantity of colour, but the effects obtained are the most brilliant of all silks.

### Figured crêpe

This can be used for all the techniques given in this book. There are several different types and the weave will affect the way the light falls on the design.

Make sure that both sides of the fabric are spread with gutta and stick to simple motifs or colour combinations which highlight the woven design.

*Example on pongé showing a cushion painted with vegetation.*

*Example on crêpe showing a cushion painted with zebras.*

# Silk paints

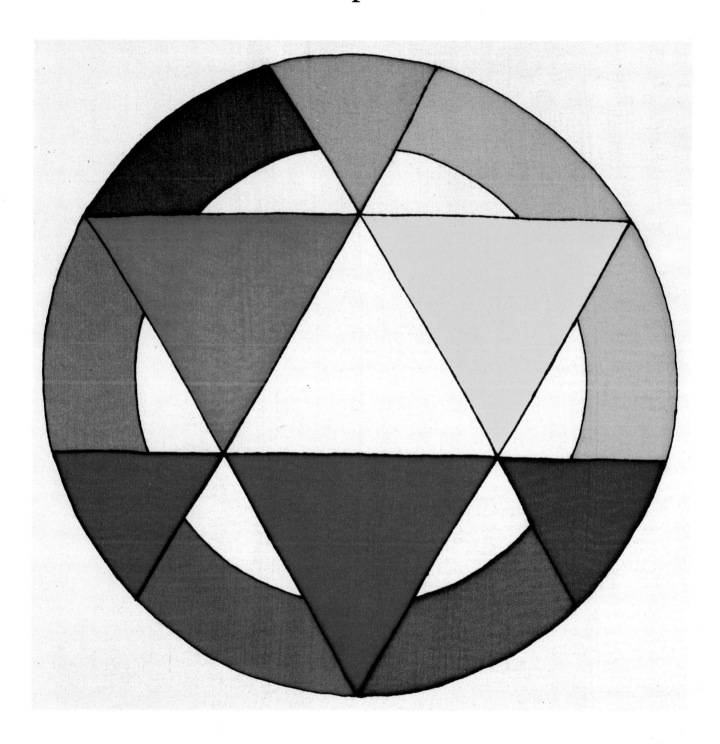

The pigments come in concentrated liquid form specially prepared for painting on silk, and there are many different types available. Some have to be diluted with water, others require a special agent produced by the paint manufacturer, but the majority can be diluted initially with a mixture of one-part pure alcohol or methylated spirits, (obtained from a chemist) to two-parts water.

When you have made your choice, prepare your working colours by placing a few drops of the concentrated paint into a watertight container and blend it with the recommended dilutant. Take note that the dilutant not only thins the paint but has an effect on the painting technique.

The beginner should start with a minimum of twelve colours, as shown in the colour-wheel. The three primary colours are red, blue and yellow and when mixed with each other they produce three secondary colours, violet, green and orange. These six then give six intermediate tints.

The paint manufacturers produce a wide range of colours, some having up to 180 different tones, and the more variety you have, the richer the effects you can achieve.

7

# Colour variations

*Colours diluted with water and alcohol.*

Colours can be mixed together, as explained on page 7, but they can also be made lighter by varying the amount of dilutant used. Be careful when applying the diluted paint, as some pigments spread smoothly, while others, which have been thinned too much, tend to show the brush marks when applied over a large surface. In this event, you need to work more rapidly, or wet the silk with water before painting.

### Colour washes
When the paint is applied to the silk, the colours will spread outwards and blend into each other. This spread can be checked by applying gutta outlines beforehand. Don't take your colour-wash right up to the edges of these masked areas, only within about 3mm (⅛in), as the paint will fill the gaps of its own accord.

To fill in a small shape, begin with a drop of colour placed in the centre of the area.

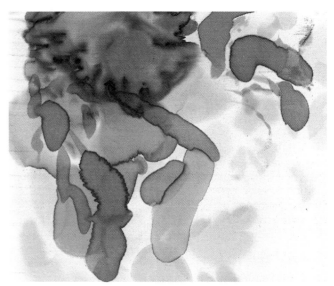

### Colour displacement
The paints used for silk painting display special characteristics and these unique properties make the results both exciting and unexpected. For example, when a wet tint is painted over an area of dried paint, which has not been outlined with gutta, a 'halo' effect may result where the two colours intersect. To correct this if the effect is unintentional, see page 13, but this phenomenon can sometimes be used to achieve very pleasing results as part of a design.

# Stretching the silk

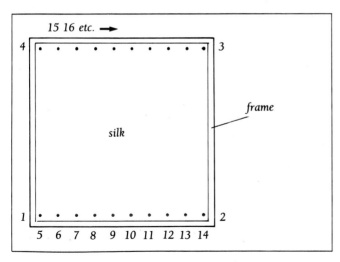

Fixing the silk to the frame
with drawing-pins.

## Basic frames

These are the most popular for stretching the silk prior to painting and are made from soft wood, usually pine, into which drawing or three-pronged pins can be fixed. You can also obtain slotted frames which can be adjusted, and fixed frames to a specific size. The silk must never be allowed to sag in the middle of the frame, or touch the surface on which the frame is supported, as the paint will collect at the lowest point.

On these frames, begin by pinning the silk at the four corners, as shown in the diagram, then continue stretching the silk and pinning it along each side at intervals of about 3 or 4cm (1¼ or 1½in) between the pins.

## Adjustable frames

On more expensive frames, the side pieces are joined by wing-nuts through holes at 5cm (2in) intervals and they can be adjusted to stretch the silk to whatever size you require. By tightening the wing-nuts you can ensure that the silk is evenly stretched and kept taut, and is also correctly suspended above the working surface.

# Techniques

## Masking with gutta

As explained on page 8, applied colour tends to spread out in all directions from the loaded brush. It can be checked by applying a masking agent, such as gutta.

Gutta, or gutta-percha to give it its full name, is a rubber derivative which is thick and colourless. It is used as a malleable agent to either outline shapes, or fill in whole areas. This glue-like substance penetrates the silk fibres, forming a barrier so that the paint cannot spread into another adjoining colour.

Gutta is normally transparent and, when it is finally removed after the silk has been painted, it will leave an outline in the same colour as the original silk. If you wish to leave a coloured outline in your design, you can colour the gutta with printing ink.

### Consistency of gutta

If the gutta is too thin, it will allow the colours to intermingle and if it is too thick, it is difficult to apply smoothly. To thicken the consistency, just add a little more undiluted gutta to the mixture. When it is too thick, you can obtain a special solvent to dilute it from craft shops. The consistency is right when the gutta forms a thin trickle as it is applied.

*Holding the gutta applicator.*

### To make an applicator

If you do not wish to go to the expense of buying a gutta applicator, see page 5, you can make an inexpensive alternative. Make a funnel from a rectangular piece of fairly

### Holding an applicator

This method is the simplest way of applying the gutta and it is easier to control than the paper funnel. After you have prepared the applicator, see page 5, fill it with gutta and hold it lightly between your thumb and forefinger, as you would a pen. Place your arm on the working surface to support it, as shown, with the applicator pointing down towards the silk.

To begin to use the gutta, apply an even and gentle pressure to the bottle to release the gutta through the nib attachment. If you are a beginner, you may experience some difficulty but problems can be remedied, see page 12.

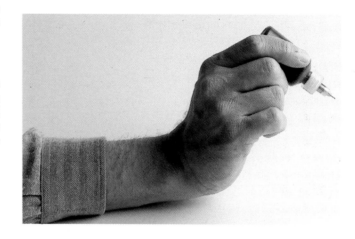

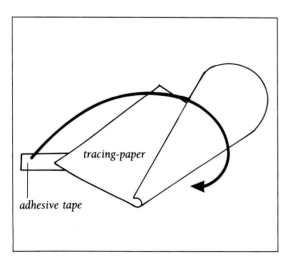

strong tracing-paper, turned on itself and fixed with adhesive tape in a cone shape, see the diagram. Leave a small opening at the narrow end and when the funnel is filled, the gutta is poured from this opening.

With this method, the gutta flows continuously from the funnel. Place a piece of cardboard with a central hole cut out over a jar and put the funnel through this hole when not in use, see above.

# Transferring the design on to silk

When the silk is thin enough, place your design underneath the stretched silk on the frame without touching it, and draw the outlines directly on to the silk. For thicker silk, you can improvise a light box by using two trestles with a sheet of glass placed on them, lit from below by a lamp.

This method can be a little difficult, but the following instructions will help you; although as with almost every art-form, only practice makes perfect.

### Drawing the design

Having placed your design beneath the silk, you can use a pencil to transfer it, but your outlines need to be very precise as the pencil marks cannot be removed from the silk.

It is safer to use a water-soluble or light-sensitive marker pen which disappears after a few hours and, therefore, can be used without anxiety. Extraneous marks will vanish or be obscured by later colour-washes.

### Drawing with gutta

To produce a steady and regular flow with the gutta, you must position your forearm on the silk. It may help if you also place a piece of clean absorbent paper underneath your arm.

Always leave an untouched area on the silk for this purpose. If you are right-handed, begin at the top-left corner and finish at the bottom-right corner, and vice-versa if you are left-handed.

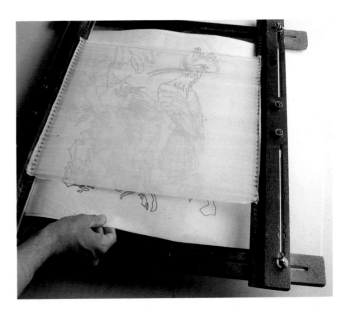

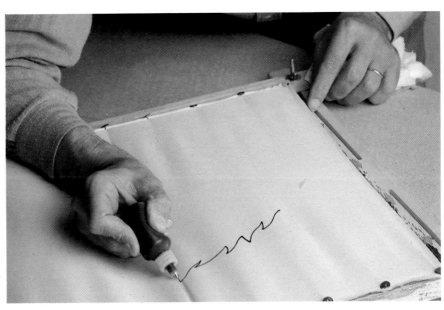

*Top: Positioning the design.*

*Middle: Drawing with a water-soluble pen.*

*Bottom: Drawing with a gutta applicator.*

# Problems with gutta

The applicator must be held at a slight angle to the surface of the silk, without pressing on it. If you hear a rasping sound as you move across the silk, then you are pressing too hard. The gutta must emerge in a steady and consistent flow.

If the outlines are not firm enough or are uneven in density, when the paint is applied it will seep through into another area of the design. You can sometimes disguise these mistakes later on, but it is much better to check before you begin to paint.

Once the gutta has dried, hold the silk up to the light to ensure that there are no gaps. Renew any lines and allow to dry again. On thicker silk you may have to apply the gutta to both sides of the fabric.

If, in spite of all your care, some colour does seep through, lighten this very gently with alcohol and remove the surplus with absorbent paper. Allow to dry and draw over the gap with fresh gutta.

### Drops of gutta

Have a piece of absorbent paper at hand to wipe away any drops of gutta on the nib or funnel, as spots dripped on to the silk will present a problem. To avoid a messy start, hold a spare piece of cloth close up to the silk and begin the gutta line on the cloth, and then go on to the silk without stopping.

*The colour breaks through the gutta.*

# Painting a large area

It is important to work very quickly, as where a wet wash joins a dry one, a 'halo' effect occurs, see page 8. The colour must be spread over the entire surface of the silk, controlling the liquid edge of the wash so as to avoid going over any dried areas already painted.

Don't begin to paint a background unless you are sure you have sufficient time to finish it and always make sure that your brush is fully loaded with paint.

Please note, that it is essential to achieve a uniform background, so use broad brush strokes and don't be tempted to go back over an area. If an area is saturated with too much colour, it will take a longer time to dry out and may result in an uneven effect.

# Fixing the paints

All painting on textiles requires fixing to make the colours permanent. Some silk paints are fixed by applying heat once they are dry, and this can be done with an ordinary iron. The best results are achieved by steam-fixing, but do check with the paint manufacturer's instructions before you begin.

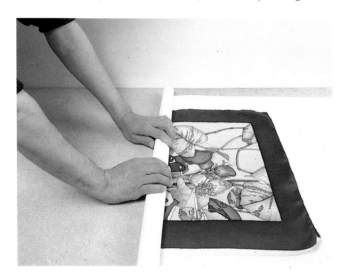

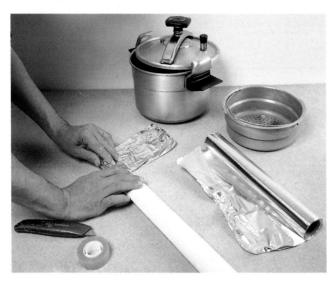

To steam-fix paints you can use a domestic pressure-cooker. First, roll the painted silk in lining paper, similar to unprinted newspaper. The whole silk surface must be in contact with the paper at all times and not with itself. Any holes in the paper may cause staining. If you have used undiluted colours, use the paper doubled. Secure the length of the paper with adhesive tape and close at both ends with aluminium foil.

Pour some water in the bottom of the pressure-cooker, place the wire basket containing the roll of silk above it, taking care that it does not come into contact with the water. Cover the basket with a protective layer of aluminium foil.

Close the pressure-cooker and leave it to steam for thirty minutes. After the silk has been fixed, wash it in cold water to remove any surplus colour.

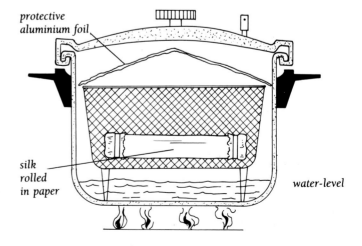

protective
aluminium foil

silk
rolled
in paper

water-level

# Professional steam-fixing

If you intend to give courses on silk painting or produce designs for sale, professional fixing equipment is available. Some specialist shops also offer a fixing service.

Three models are illustrated above: a household drier, which will take a 60cm (23½in) length of silk; one which can hold a 90cm (35½in) length and an upright model, which can fix more than 2m (2¼yds) at one time.

The household fixers are used horizontally and can be placed on a domestic cooker, but the upright one is powered by electricity. Your stockist will advise you on the best model for your requirements.

## Protecting and washing silk

All fixed silk can be washed. It may tint the water the first time, but this is merely surplus colour. Wash in lukewarm water into which a little mild soap has been dissolved.

Painted silk is light-sensitive and will fade when it is exposed to bright light, so do not hang a wall panel facing direct sunlight.

# Painting with watercolours

When using watercolours, always work on silk which is stretched taut without any creases, or the colours will gather and mix in the folds.

Go over the main lines of your drawing with pencils which are indelible and will not run or smudge.

Wet the silk with a thick brush. It must remain damp throughout the painting process.

Begin by putting in your main areas of colour but not too heavily. If one colour seems a little too strong, lighten it by diluting it with a little water. *Gradually* strengthen your tints. Keep an eye on the whole design to ensure that the colours are not displaced and that no area has dried out.

Once the silk is on the point of drying out, put in your strongest shading. This avoids the risk of your colours running.

*Top: Wetting the silk.*

*Middle: Laying on the colours.*

*Bottom: The finished painting.*

# Salt technique

This simple technique produces exciting and unexpected results. By a chemical phenomenon, salt grains absorb the pigment content of the paints to form dark outlines, rings, streaks or abstract shapes.

The salt may be applied to wet or dry silk, but for the latter method, grains of salt are placed on the dry silk and then paint is brushed directly on to them. The easiest way is to first wet the silk all over with clean water. Prepare a range of two to three colours which have not been diluted and mix them indiscriminately on the silk.

Now take a handful of salt grains and sprinkle them over the wet colours, but do not use too many. Leave to dry, then lightly brush off the saturated grains. The tints will take longer to dry out but will give a more brilliant, if unpredictable, result.

*Top: Place the paints on the wet silk.*

*Middle: Position the grains of salt.*

*Bottom: The finished results.*

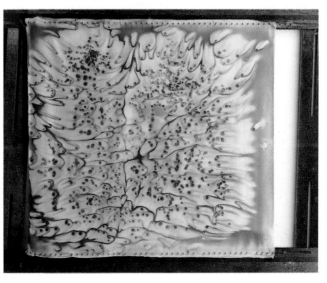

# Effects with alcohol

Place a drop of pure undiluted alcohol on top of your background tint. This will lighten the effect leaving around the drop of alcohol a border of deeper colour.

If required, the process can be repeated once the paint is dry to lighten the effect still further. A few extra droplets round the first mark will provide the flower effect illustrated here.

# Direct painting

This is one of the most difficult and delicate techniques, as you paint directly on to the *dry* silk, first the pale washes, then the deeper ones. Prepare your range of pure, or slightly diluted colours and keep your design beside you for reference.

Having put in your main colour areas, leave to dry. Take a very fine brush and have a piece of rag available for wiping the brush clean. Dip the point in a little pigment and begin to add the minute details.

Be warned. This method allows for no mistakes and a carelessly placed colour cannot be removed.

# Anti-fusant method

This is a simple technique which dispenses with the need for gutta outlines. Anti-fusant solutions are supplied by the paint manufacturers, and these can be brushed on to the silk either as an all-over background, or in small, separate areas.

Take the brush and apply a layer of anti-fusant over the well-stretched silk. Once this is dry, position your design underneath the silk and trace it in with coloured pencils.

Now wash in your colours, which should not run into each other. While the washes remain wet, you can introduce gradations, if required.

Be warned. Wait until one colour is completely dry before applying a colour next to it, just in case the colours intermix.

When the painting is finished, you will notice that the anti-fusant tends to stiffen the silk. After the paints have been fixed, you can soften the silk by placing it in a benzine solution. Wash and rinse the silk thoroughly.

*Top: Applying the anti-fusant.*

*Middle: Applying the paints.*

*Bottom: The finished painting.*

# Gallery of designs

The full colour range for each design is given, see the silk samples below, together with a chart which you can enlarge to suit your requirements, see page 4. As an example, the squares on the grid of the motifs each measure 1.5cm (⅝in).

To obtain the size for the motif on the panel opposite, each square should be enlarged to 10cm (4in), noting that extra material is allowed for mounting, to give a full size of 125 × 91cm (49¼ × 35¾in).

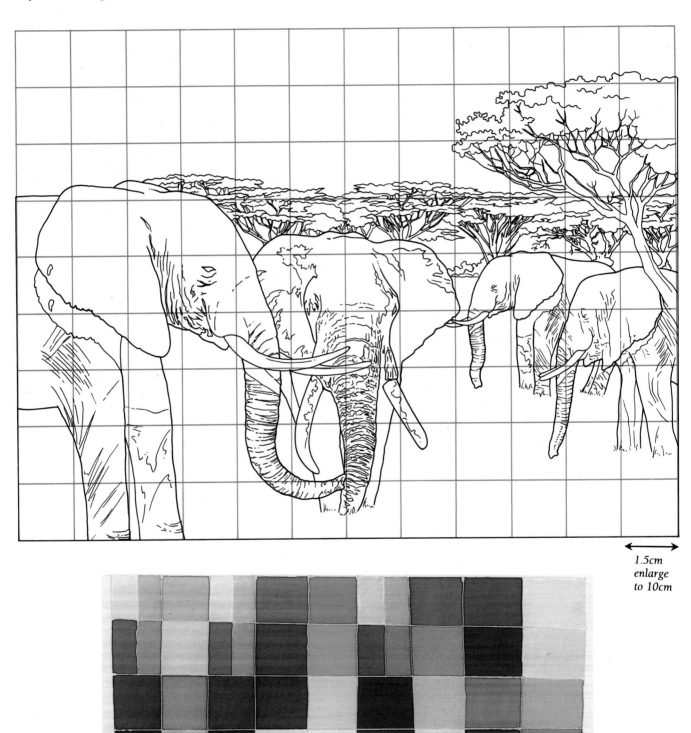

*1.5cm enlarge to 10cm*

# Elephants-panel

*Silk pongé No. 9 – full size 125 × 91cm (49¼ × 35¾in).*

Strength, massiveness and calmness are the features depicted in this elephant design. The strength is suggested by the central elephant and the tusks on either side of him break up the triangular composition.

A feeling of mass is provided by the elephant in the foreground. Although only partially represented, it occupies a quarter of the panel. The jungle in the distance also emphasizes the giant scale of the elephants.

The general colouring gives a very calming effect. There are no warm tones, only combinations of grey, grey-blue and grey-purple, as well as a rich range of greens from grass-green to olive, with very pale blue for the sky. Do not use any warm colours, such as yellow, orange or red in this design.

Apply black gutta outlines for the elephants and the foliage. To define the tree branches over a very deep, olive-green background for the jungle, use transparent gutta.

The elephants are painted in four shades of grey, see the illustrated samples. The sky, which is very light, must be rapidly washed in to avoid brush marks.

The foreground elephant on the left, requires thick brushes; the shading should be wet-on-wet, as given for the technique of watercolours on silk, see page 16.

For the grass, paint in the background tint first. Leave to dry, then finish with direct painting, as given for the Zebra design, see page 37.

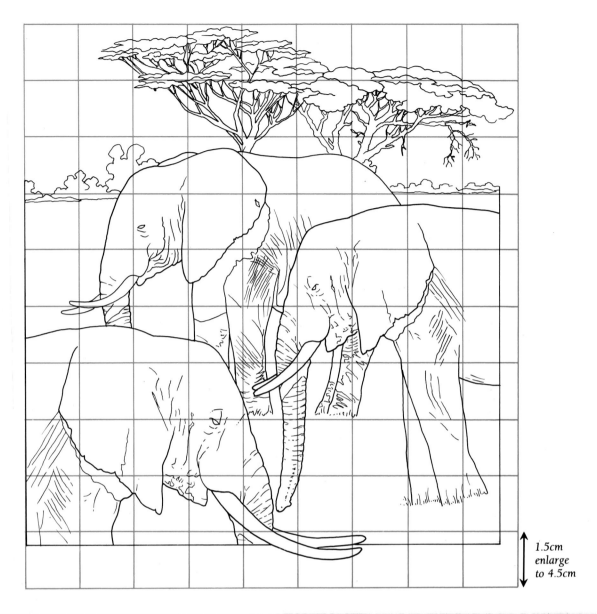

1.5cm
enlarge
to 4.5cm

# Elephants-scarf

*Silk pongé No. 7 – full size 160 × 40cm (63 × 15¾in).*
*Fringed and hemmed by hand.*

Study the colour range carefully. You will need three basic tints: black, violet and garnet-red. The other shades are obtained by mixing these colours. The whole design is first drawn in with black or grey gutta.

The elephants are worked in a range of grey-violets. To overcome a flat effect, introduce gradations of tone wet-on-wet.

The grass and trees should be worked in more reddish colours. For the lower edge of the motif representing the grass, use a very diluted colour, with *one* unit of pigment to *five* of alcohol plus water. For the full range of colours, see the silk samples opposite.

The branches are fairly dark, using the same purple-grey tints as for the elephants. They need to stand out from the background.

For the background, prepare a little lilac hue by mixing the grey-violet of the elephants with the garnet-red of the foliage. Prepare four gradated shades of this by diluting varying strengths, shading to a very pale tone for the final one.

Wet the scarf thoroughly omitting the design area, then apply the total of five shades over the damp background. Mix them well in where they blend to avoid hard edges.

1.5cm
enlarge
to 4.5cm

# Elephants-cushion

*Silk pongé No. 10 – full size to cover a cushion 43 × 43cm (17 × 17in).*

The philodendron border, with its silhouetted effect, provides a frame for the series of cushion covers. Only the central elephant is featured here, but you can use any part of the motif given on page 20.

To begin, draw in all the outlines with gutta extending the contours of the last leaf at the bottom right. It will be easier to paint the border once the risk of any unevenness, or halo effect, is reduced. The garnet-red tint of the outline sets off the light tones of the grass and sky.

The gutta not only checks the spread of the colours but can be used as a pencil to draw in details. For the wrinkles on the elephant's trunk, mask in the black lines and, when colouring, enhance the line with a deeper shade applied with the point of the brush.

For the head and the trunk, first paint in the light areas with three shades of grey, to suggest the modelling of the body and ears. Leave to dry, then add the deeper tones within the gutta outlines.

25

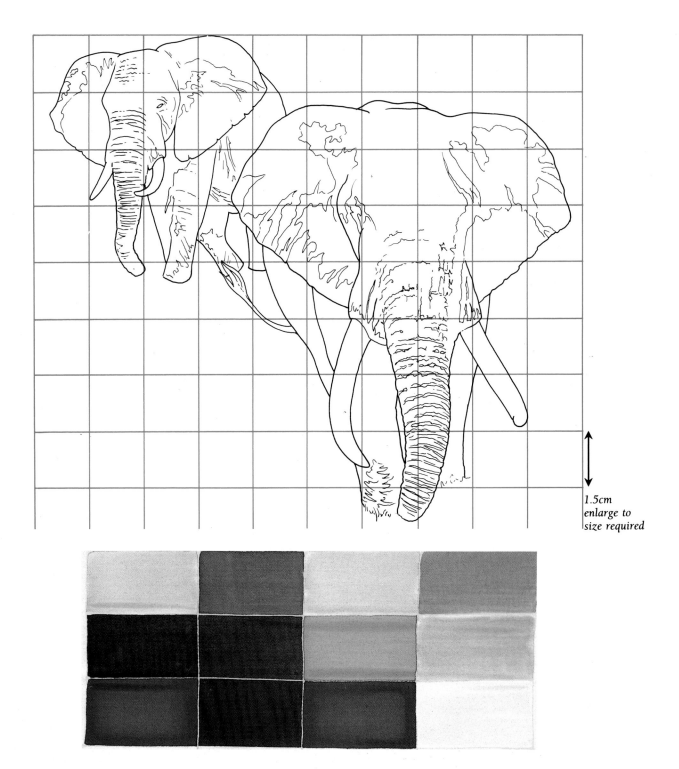

1.5cm
enlarge to
size required

This blouse or T-shirt, is lined with white twill, which strengthens the silk and also enhances the brightness of your colours.

It is designed for a small boy and painted in cold hues of blue and grey.

Working on crêpe de Chine involves few difficulties, as with pongé No. 10.

First, place your pattern front and back on to the silk and trace out the shape, allowing an extra 2cm (¾in) on each side edge, and at the top and lower edges for seaming. Draw in your design on the front with black gutta. The background and also the back of the blouse features small elephants placed at random. Paint in the two large ones with grey,

using blue for the smaller ones. Add small accents of deeper blue under the ears with the tip of the brush.

It is important to begin by drawing the design with gutta, in order to ensure that the gutta penetrates the silk. If there are any accidental marks, then these will be hidden by the deeper background painted in later.

Use the water and alcohol method for this background, see page 18. Prepare a jar of blue tint and a second of black. Paint with a free, rich mix of these colours, then leave to dry for half an hour.

With a mixture of water and alcohol, apply some droplets of the liquid from your brush which will dilute the colours, see page 18. This can be repeated, if required, after drying.

26

# Elephants-child's top

*Crêpe de Chine – to fit a five-year old.*

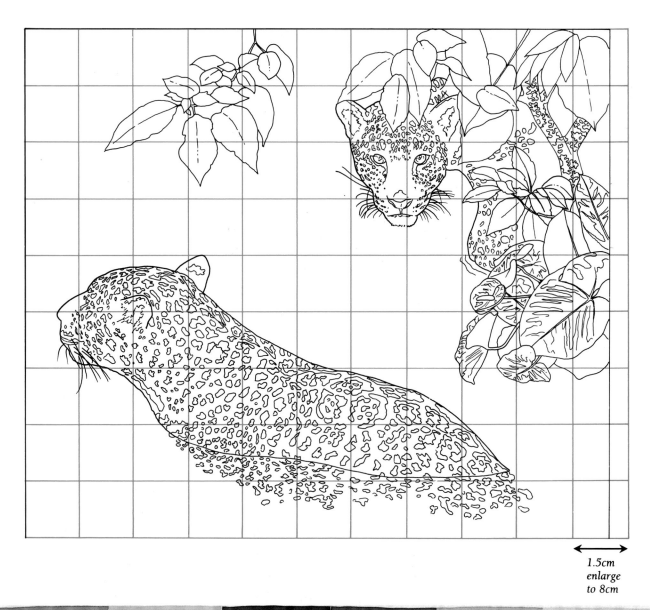

1.5cm
enlarge
to 8cm

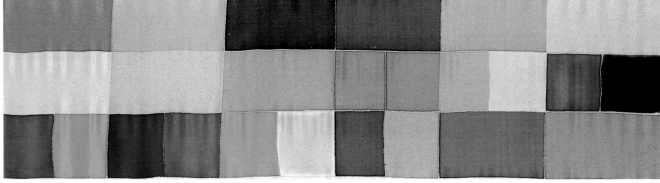

The leopards are drawn in black gutta, including the spots, with the exception of the whiskers, which are in transparent gutta. The leaves are in green gutta and the branch in a reddish-brown gutta.

Prepare the colour for the bodies of the leopards, mixing an orange tint with a drop of maroon. Dilute it into three separate pots: dark, medium and light.

Begin with the leopard in the foreground. Having made sure the gutta is dry, wash in the lightest tint over the lowest part of the animal, without worrying about the black spots on the leopard which will be applied later. Moving upwards, place the medium tint and, right at the top, the darkest shade. The variation in colour will give the leopard a feeling of mass. With a dry brush, blend your colours into each other avoiding 'haloes'. This should be done quite quickly.

For the top leopard, use an alcohol-plus-water mix as your

# Wild cats-panel

*Silk pongé No. 9 – full size 87cm (34¼in) wide × 84cm (33in) deep.*

fourth colour, to preserve the white areas beneath the eyes and the white muzzle.

To make the washing in of the background easier, introduce a line of black gutta between the last leaf and the bottom leopard. Prepare a good measure of olive-green.

When the colour is ready, prepare five mixes with the background tint plus the orange hue used for the leopards. This should be gradated from the olive-green towards the reddish-brown and progressively lightened to produce the reflections under the bodies.

Take a thick brush. Begin to paint in the background in a line between the leaf and the leopard, rising towards the top left. Be sure to dampen your background well, see page 13 for painting a uniform background.

Having reached the leopard in the foreground, use your prepared tones to create the reflections. Paint in the black spots on the leopards, and finish off your background against the line of gutta from which you began.

When all is dry, go over the leopards' spots again with black, plus their reflections in the water.

Be warned. The painting of the background and reflections is the *hardest* task set in this book!

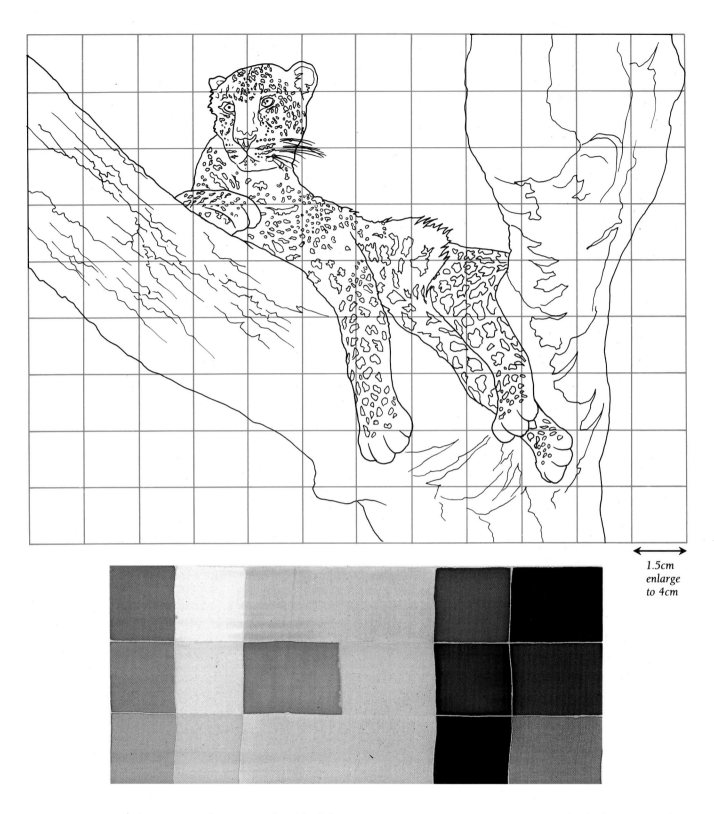

1.5cm
enlarge
to 4cm

The design is painted on a rectangle 39cm (15¼in) high by 77.5cm (30in) long, noting that the motif does not go all the way round the circumference.

Draw the whole motif in black gutta, including the spots, whiskers and branches. Once the gutta is dry, prepare the gradation of colours for the leopard. Apply the lightest hue over the whole area, not worrying about the black spots, then rapidly add the deeper colours over a wet base so that a smooth transition is achieved.

Be sure to place the shadows accurately. For instance, the folded paw beneath the head must be light, and the fur behind darker, to give the correct perspective.

When everything is dry, paint in the black spots. The blue background must be laid on fairly rapidly to avoid leaving brush marks, shading from dark at the top to azure on the lower edge.

For the bark of the tree, use the gutta again like a pencil. Make black lines, to be strengthened by touches of the brush when painting. Remember when painting the tree, to put in a dark brown beneath the leopard to suggest its shadow.

# Wild cats-lampshade

*Silk pongé No. 7 – cylindrical shade 39cm (15¼in) high × 25cm (9¾in) diameter.*

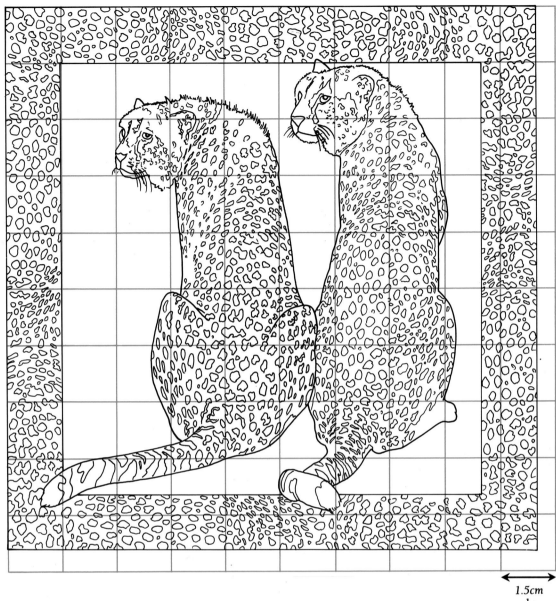

1.5cm
*enlarge
to 9cm*

# Wild cats-square scarf

*Twill – full size 90 × 90cm (35½ × 35½in). Hand rolled hem.*

The colour range of this square scarf is very simple. Reddish-brown for the cheetahs, lightened in four gradations, a redder and deeper brown for the background, and this last colour also lightened for the surround. Finally, some black for the spots, a drop of blue for the eyes, and a spot of red for the noses.

Use black gutta to draw the design and transparent gutta if you wish to add your signature.

Unlike some of the previous examples, success depends here on the effective 'modelling' of the cheetahs' bodies. The gradations of tone should be made over the *dried* gutta which will require at least a full day. Prepare the colour for the cheetahs, mixing orange-yellow with a reddish-brown, then dilute this into *five* shades from very light to dark.

With a thick brush, spread your lightest shade over the whole cheetah. On this wet wash, place stronger tints to build up your gradations and on the masked area, put in the inside spots, which will be painted in at the end when all is dry. Use intermediate colours to soften your gradations. Place the deepest shade over the spine and the lighter tones round the edges.

Throughout, the whole cheetah area must remain wet. If need be, dampen any part that threatens to dry out.

1.5cm
enlarge
to 4cm

# Wild cats-cushion

*Silk pongé No. 9 – full size to cover a cushion 43 × 43cm (17 × 17in).*

The philodendron silhouette motif, used for the cushion on page 25, would have detracted from the effect of the lion's head, and so is not employed here. Instead, the animal's mane overlaps a conventional border.

Note that black gutta must be used for the whole of the design, except for transparent gutta to define the whiskers above the eyebrows.

The bright red background accentuates the ferocity of the roaring lion, while his coat should be painted in soft muted shades. Paint the head with the lightest hue and keep the strongest ones for the muzzle and lips, to be detailed with the tip of the brush.

The colour for the mane is a mix of the dark brown used for the border, and the background red. Four tones will be required, from the deepest to the lightest.

1.5cm
enlarge
to 9cm

# Zebras-panel

*Silk pongé No. 9 – full size 112 × 88cm (45 × 35in) allowing for sky area.*

The zebras are masked in black gutta, the trees in reddish-brown and the foliage in green gutta. Having applied the gutta, leave it to dry for a full day.

Begin by painting the sky. The light blue isn't very easy to wash in and if you follow the outlines of the foilage too closely, you risk making obtrusive brush marks. It is better, therefore, to use a thick brush and rapidly go over the whole sky surface, including the trees and their trunks. Such a pale tint will not affect the greens and browns to be painted in later.

To paint the zebras, see the instructions given on the following pages.

For the foreground area, wash in the basic creamy-beige shade rapidly, with a large brush, or prepared brushes. Vary the surface slightly to avoid too monotonous an effect. Leave this background to dry thoroughly. Take a thin brush, and with a little colour on it, depict the tufts of grass in tiny, quick strokes in shades of reddish-brown, olive-green, grass-green, and so on, noting that the more gradations you use, the more realistic the result.

Pay particular attention to the relative proportions and the way in which the foreground recedes into the distance. The grasses should be progressively reduced in height and definition towards the distance, but should appear much larger and stronger in the foreground.

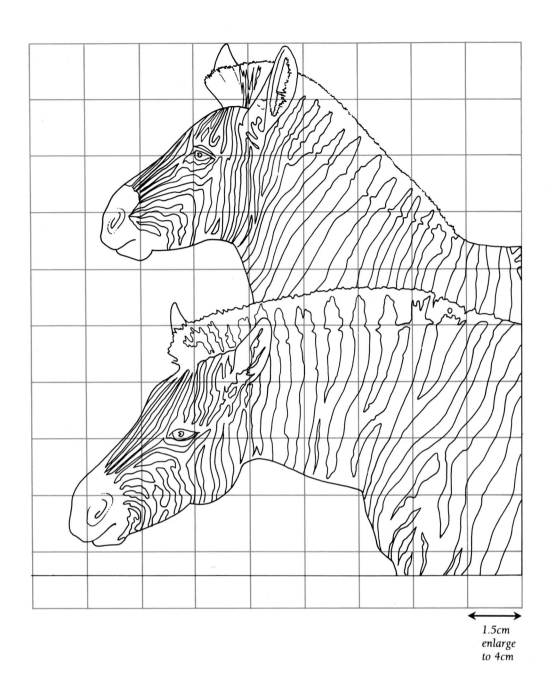

1.5cm
enlarge
to 4cm

# Zebras-scarf

*Silk pongé No. 7 – full size 160 × 40cm (63 × 15¾in).*

For this scarf, the whole design must be traced in black gutta, except for the nostrils and the mouths, which are worked in transparent gutta. Leave the gutta to dry thoroughly before beginning the next stage.

Prepare three jars, the first containing a mixture of water plus alcohol, the second with a touch of grey, and the third a little more grey.

Begin with the head in the foreground. Brush in the water-plus-alcohol mix over the head and neck of the animal, then shade in under the head and neck with a light grey and finally, add the stronger grey right at the lower edge of the head and neck. Try to blend your tones into one another. The shadow areas need to be very light and muted with no hard edges. Before this dries, place a touch of grey on the tips of the ears.

Using the same colours, paint in the second animal. The shadow tone should be placed beneath the head and over the neck for the length of the first zebra's mane. Once everything is thoroughly dry, paint in the stripes, manes, muzzles and eyes.

Be careful. The background must be smoothly painted, see page 13, in a shade of dark grey. The tinting of the lower edging is a diluted tone of the same grey.

1.5cm
enlarge
to 4cm

# Zebras-cushion

*Figured crêpe – full size to cover a cushion 43 × 43cm (17 × 17in).*

The whole design is worked in black gutta. Spreading the gutta on this figured crêpe, which has a satin finish, is the main problem. In fact, this material is patterned all over with a design in relief, and the gutta must not only cover it, but also be applied on the reverse side. This is a longish process, but it will pay dividends later!

There are no further difficulties. Work the zebras as in the previous examples, with a light shadow beneath the heads and under the throats and stomachs.

Once the material is dry, apply the black stripes and the light blue background. The silhouetted edging is worked in a darker blue. The background is the same colour as the border, but diluted with a mixture of water plus alcohol.

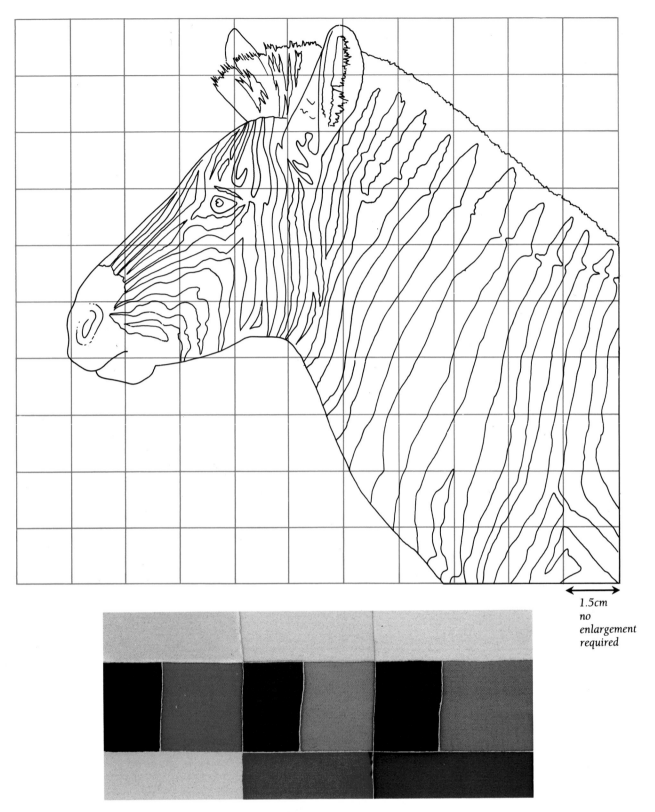

1.5cm
*no*
*enlargement*
*required*

These nursery panels are constructed on the principle of bright, contrasting tints, such as green and red, and orange and blue, which are complementary colours, see page 7.

Use black gutta to transfer the zebra design, apart from the mouth and the white of the eye, for which transparent gutta is required.

Leave the gutta to dry thoroughly, then prepare three shades of blue: very light, medium, and one slightly stronger, for the centre panel of the series. Continue as for the scarf,

see page 39. Wash in the lightest tone at the top, the medium towards the centre and the deepest towards the base. When your gradation dries out paint the zebras black, then the background in vivid yellow.

Vary the colours for the zebras, as shown, on the panels with red and blue backgrounds.

In order to frame silk paintings, it is advisable to place felt stripping along the background edges. Use double-sided adhesive tape to attach the silk to a cardboard backing.

# Zebras-nursery panels

*Silk pongé No. 5 – full size 23 × 34cm (9 × 13½in).*

1.5cm
enlarge
to 9.5cm

# Vegetation-panel

*Silk pongé No. 9 – full size 116 × 80cm (46½ × 31½in).*

Apart from the black background, three-quarters of the colours used on this panel are derived from a range of greens. You will be able to use this opportunity to the full, to achieve the varied colour mixing which is possible in silk painting, from green-yellow, through green-brown to green-blue. The original design used nine basic greens, as well as their diluted gradations.

Before beginning your preparations, take note of an optical phenomenon which is very important in this design. Warm tints, such as red and yellow, appear to advance into the foreground, while cooler ones, such as blue and green, appear to retreat into the background. To make the leaves in the foreground stand out, use a bright yellow. The masking is done throughout with black gutta.

45

The salient feature of the panel is its central area adorned by the two large, colourful leaves. Begin with these.

Prepare a tonal range of five yellowish-green hues, the lightest almost colourless. Place these gradated tones, from the lightest to medium, along the leaf edges. Before this dries, mark in the principal vein-structures with the tip of the brush.

# Vegetation-scarf

*Silk pongé No. 9 – full size 160 × 40cm (63 × 15¾in).*

Designed for a scarf, this motif, suitably enlarged, would make an ideal wall panel.

Use black gutta for the whole design, except for the silhouetted effect of the palm-trees, where the masking is in green.

The more luminous foreground tints, grass-green and yellow-green, are set off by the olive background to which a touch of brown may be added. The leaves and palm-trees of the foreground should be gradated in tone to give them perspective.

For the pale orange background, use the same technique as given for the scarf on page 23. Prepare your base colour, mixing orange plus a few drops of reddish-brown, and dilute to make three lighter tones. Spread water over the whole surface with a large brush, except for the design itself, then paint in the orange washes, intermingling them well. Wetting the scarf will enable you to work more confidently, without running a risk of unevenness.

*1.5cm enlarge to size required*

This simple skirt and sleeveless top does not really need a paper pattern. When the painting is completed, the skirt can be cut in one piece and seamed at the centre back, leaving an opening at the top, then gathered at the top and a waistband added. Finally, hem the lower edge. The top is also a basic shape and can be lined, see the design on page 26.

The philodendron silhouette design, shown on the cushion on page 25, shows up the texture and translucency of the fabric to great effect. Draw in the gutta outlines on the fabric, allowing a margin of 2cm (¾in) for seaming. Use

black gutta, then turn the silk to the reverse side and repeat the design. Leave to dry thoroughly for a full day.

Prepare the gradations of colour, beginning with light blue at the lower edge and apply the paint without bothering about the gutta. When the colour dries, you may be wise to add colourless gutta over the blue and against the black gutta.

Paint in the darkest blue with a well-saturated brush to avoid a halo effect.

52

# Vegetation-girl's skirt and top

*Figured crêpe.*

1.5cm
enlarge
to 8cm

# Birds-panel

*Silk pongé No. 9 – full size 100 × 72cm (39½ × 28¼in).*

If you enjoy preparing and mixing colours, then this design
will be a challenge and will afford you a great deal of
pleasure.

Though the effect is well-balanced, this panel is conceived
in two distinct parts; the left-hand side using the motif for
the lampshade, see page 60 for the complete motif, with two
parrots to the right, see page 57 for details. The instructions
for painting the birds are given in the following pages.

For this panel, it is the background which gives unity to
the whole effect. Mix an almond-green with a few drops of
brown and dilute with water plus alcohol. Don't rush it,
above all, leave the paint to dry well in order to be certain
that you have the shade you want. You can always initially
make the shade slightly lighter or darker than the one shown
here.

The whole design is drawn in black gutta, with the
exception of the left-hand birds, which are more deeply
tinted. Use transparent gutta here, in order to make the
drawing of the feathers stand out. Also, use transparent gutta
for the points of light on the beak, the throat of the
foreground bird and the highlight in the eye.

The painting of the foreground bird depends on two basic
hues; navy blue and bright red. Add a few drops of blue to the
red, and red to the blue. You will thus achieve a slightly
violet shade, which will complement both primary colours.

For the bird in the background, paint the beak, ruffles and
plumage in much lighter tones.

# The parrots

These provide excellent practice in gradating colours. The red of the left-hand parrot, for instance, is made up of a mixture of pink, red, and reddish-brown.

Paint in the pink first, then the red, mixing it into the pink before this dries. Now, with the tip of the brush add the reddish-brown shadows.

Continue with the yellow feathers in a clear lemon yellow and, before it dries, add a drop of green to the edges of the feathers with the tip of the brush. Complete the lower feathers with blue.

The same attention to colour blending is required for the right-hand parrot. The basic colour for the body is a lively blue, almost turquoise. A very light shade of this will do for the lower feathers.

1.5cm
enlarge
to 4.5cm

# Birds-cushion

*Silk pongé No. 9 – full size to cover a cushion 43 × 43cm (17 × 17in).*

Use black gutta to draw in the design, except for the tail feathers of the large bird, which require transparent gutta.

Begin by drawing the head of the large bird. The crest, which overlaps the border area, should also be masked before tracing in the extent of the interior square. Complete all the gutta, beginning at the top-left corner and working to the bottom-right corner if you are right-handed, and vice-versa, if left-handed.

This cushion presents few problems. The colour of the border is a mixture of black and violet and by lightening this hue, you will also obtain the pale purple of the background.

For the white plumage of the large bird, prepare a jar of water plus alcohol and another containing very light blue. Lay in the water and alcohol mixture over the silk, and into it place a few drops of the blue at random with the tip of your brush.

To enliven the tree bark, draw in little lines with a fine brush and a minimum of colour.

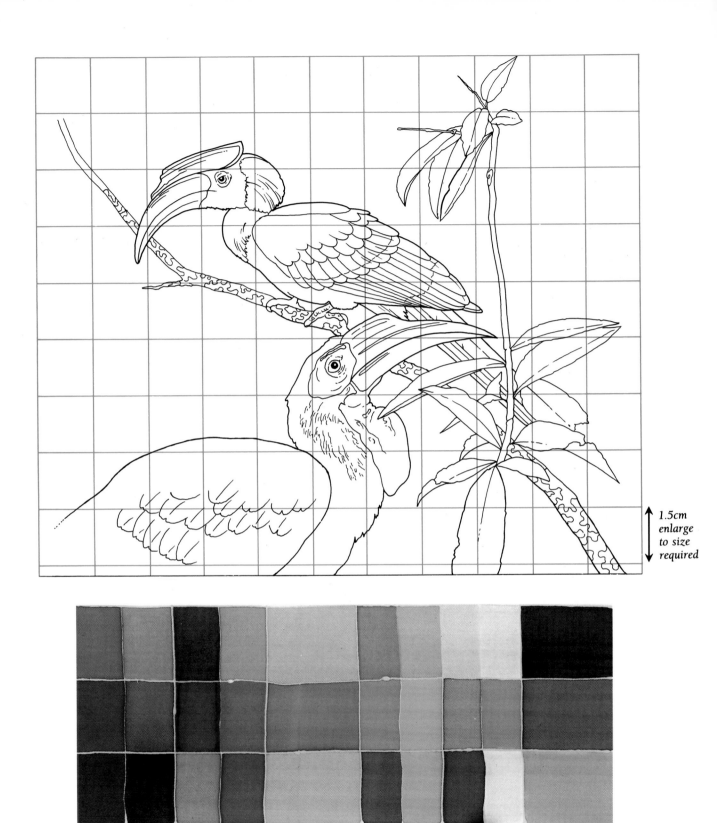

1.5cm
enlarge
to size
required

The corners of this lampshade are rounded. The simplest way to measure the circumference to arrive at the length of fabric you require, is to place a tape-measure on a firm surface and secure it at each end with drawing-pins. Mark the beginning of the frame and place this on the tape-measure, then roll it across the tape until you arrive at the same point. In this design, the measurements will be 35 × 92cm (13¾ × 36¼in), noting that the silk is only painted over two panels of the shade.

Transfer the design on to the silk and inside this rectangle, trace your drawing with gutta. Colour the birds as for the panel given on page 56.

The neutral, light-brown tint for the background, is obtained by mixing the colour used for the beak of the bird in the foreground with the bright green used for the foliage. The whole area should be lightened with water plus alcohol, using one unit of paint to seven of dilutant.

# Birds-lampshade

*Silk pongé No. 7 – full size 35cm (13¾in) high × 25cm (9¾in) diameter.*

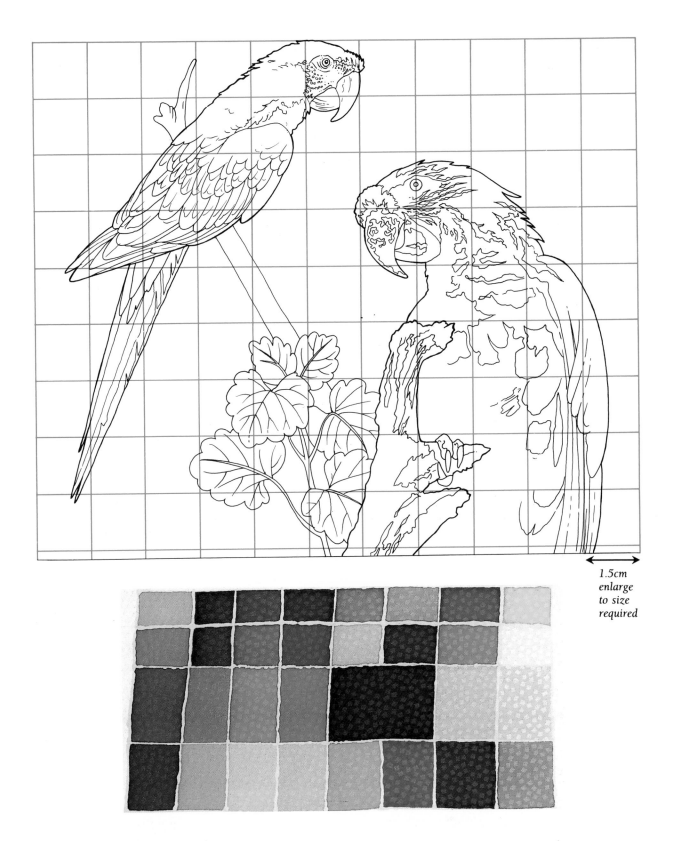

*1.5cm*
*enlarge*
*to size*
*required*

Begin by drawing your pattern pieces on to the silk, leaving 2cm (¾in) on each side for seaming. As already explained on pages 41 and 52, the gutta has to be applied to *both* sides of the material to make sure it penetrates.

Don't be afraid to make your masking lines quite strong, especially on the boundaries between the motif and the background. As the latter is very dark, any evidence of the gutta will not be noticed.

Now begin to paint the design. The gradations are prepared in the same way as for working on pongé, see page 57, only the pigment takes longer to apply and penetrate the fabric.

Be very careful when painting the background as this type of material is a perfect sponge! It absorbs twice as much colour as a normal silk, so prepare plenty, as it is difficult to match the exact colour again.

# Birds-woman's top
*Figured crêpe*

# OTHER SILK PAINTING BOOKS PUBLISHED BY SEARCH PRESS

## A Complete Guide to Silk Painting
*Susanne Hahn*

This definitive guide to silk painting is a unique treasury of ideas, designs and techniques that follows the 'Silk Road' of discovery from fibre through to fabric, and takes you step by step through the different techniques of this fascinating art. Inside you will find beautiful colour illustrations detailing the history of the silk trade in Asia and Europe and the development of the modern silk-making process. There is also information and advice on materials and equipment, and many ideas for gift and home-furnishing projects, as well as examples of wall hangings, pictures and designer clothing.

## The Art of Painting on Silk
Volume 1
*Edited by Pam Dawson*

This book describes the basic techniques, tools and materials, required to paint on silk, followed by colourful examples of designs and finished items that will be useful to both the beginner and experienced artist. Useful motifs to trace are given in the final section of the book.

## The Art of Painting on Silk
Volume 2 – Soft Furnishings
*Edited by Pam Dawson*

A colourful and inspirational book which covers a wide range of soft furnishing designs, from cushions and wall hangings to bed covers and lampshades. Each design is shown in full colour together with details of materials required, methods used and simple-to-follow charts of the painted motifs.

## The Art of Painting on Silk
Volume 3 – Fashions
*Edited by Pam Dawson*

Volume three in the silk painting series gives plenty of practical advice on how to apply designs to stunning silk fashion garments. The book is full of colourful illustrations showing scarves, blouses, jackets, childrens' and babies' wear and a beautiful wedding dress, each with its own charted design.

## The Art of Painting on Silk
Volume 4 – Potpourri
*Edited by Pam Dawson*

Simple and more complex designs are colourfully illustrated and accompanied by easy-to-follow charts showing motifs for greeting cards, wall hangings, shawls, scarves, lavender bags, cushions, accessories, neckties and paintings.

## How to Paint on Silk
Abridged edition of The Art of Painting on Silk: Volume One.
*Edited by Pam Dawson*

Create beautiful gifts with this simple and colourful guide to painting on silk; greetings cards, brooches, cushions, pictures and scarves.

## Painting Flowers on Silk
Daisies, roses, irises, poppies and convolvulus
*Lydie Ottelart*

This stunning and practical book is for silk painters who want to develop their skill and produce innovative floral designs. The book begins with an important and useful section on how to draw flowers and includes many floral motifs which can easily be traced. The author illustrates unusual techniques, such as hot wax, stencilling and sugar syrup methods, and using colour, silver or gold guttas and watercolours are also illustrated. There are colour illustrations of finished items such as cushions, scarves, paintings, tablecloths and a nightgown.

## Inspirational Silk Painting from Nature
*Renate Henge*

This book will be a source of inspiration to silk painters who wish to create their own original designs. Beginning with a reminder of the various techniques which can be used in silk painting, there follows a gallery of full-colour photographs from nature and examples of finished silk paintings. Subjects covered include the sea and sky, landscapes, trees, fruit and vegetables.

Silk painting can now be enjoyed by everyone with the help of the Silk Painting Starter Kit produced jointly by Search Press and George Weil & Sons, silk materials and fabric paint suppliers. It includes five bottles of silk paint in assorted colours, a wooden frame, an outliner nib, a bottle of outliner resist, a half-metre of pure silk and a copy of *The Art of Painting on Silk*.

If you are interested in any of the above books or any of the art and craft titles published by Search Press, then please send for a free catalogue to:

**SEARCH PRESS LTD.**

Dept. B, Wellwood,
North Farm Road, Tunbridge Wells,
Kent TN2 3DR